10 9 8 7 6 5 4 3 2 1
Copyright © 2025 Carine MacKenzie
ISBN: 978-1-5271-1214-8

Published by Christian Focus Publications,
Geanies House, Fearn, Tain, Ross-shire, IV20 1TW, U.K.

Illustrations by Daniele Fabbri.
Printed and bound by Imprint, India.

Scripture quotations are author's own paraphrases, unless otherwise stated.

All rights reserved. No part of this publication may be reproduced, stored in a retrieval system, or transmitted, in any form, by any means, electronic, mechanical, photocopying, recording or otherwise without the prior permission of the publisher or a licence permitting restricted copying. In the U.K. such licences are issued by the Copyright Licensing Agency, 4 Battlebridge Lane, London, SE1 2HX. www.cla.co.uk

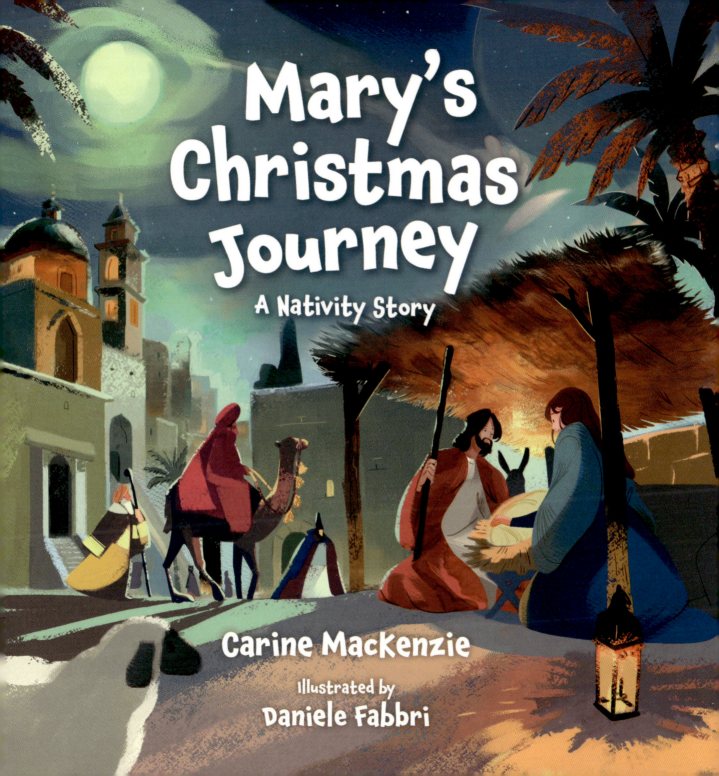

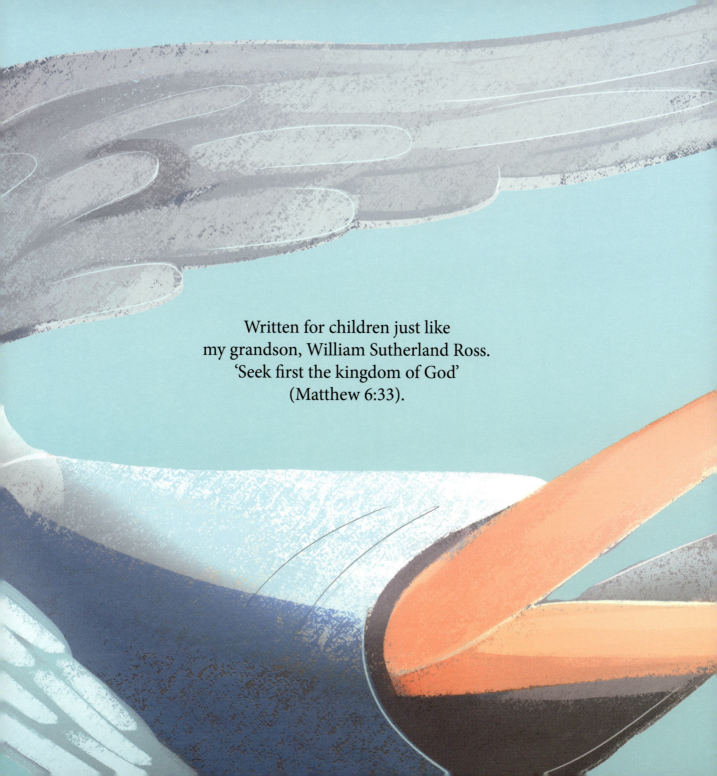

Written for children just like
my grandson, William Sutherland Ross.
'Seek first the kingdom of God'
(Matthew 6:33).

In the beginning, God made the world – a perfect, sinless world. However, sin entered that world and it had to be punished with death.

Thankfully, God made a promise. One day, he would send a Saviour from heaven to earth to defeat death and crush evil. Alongside this, another journey had to happen.

A young woman called Mary was chosen by God. An angel gave her startling news: 'You are going to have a baby boy. You will call his name Jesus. He will be great and will be called the Son of the Most High.'

'How can this happen,' said Mary, 'since I am a virgin?'
The angel replied, 'The baby is the Son of God. You will have this child by the power of God, the Holy Spirit.'

So Mary went on her first journey to visit her cousin Elizabeth in the hill country of Judea. Elizabeth was also expecting a baby even though she was quite old.

As soon as Mary entered the house, the baby inside Elizabeth jumped for joy. Elizabeth called out, 'Blessed are you among women and blessed is the baby you are bearing!'

Mary then exclaimed,
'My soul praises the Lord, and rejoices in God my Saviour.'

When Mary's fiancé, Joseph, heard about her pregnancy, he was troubled. He knew the baby was not his so he decided to break their engagement.

But then an angel spoke to him in a dream:
'Do not be afraid to take Mary as your wife, for her child was conceived by the power of the Holy Spirit. She will give birth to a son and you shall call his name Jesus for he shall save his people from their sins.'

Joseph went ahead and married Mary. Then Joseph had to go back to his home town to be counted in the census. Mary had to travel with him all the way from Nazareth to Bethlehem – a journey which would have taken them several days on foot.

Bethlehem was so busy, there wasn't even a room in which they could stay the night. Mary and Joseph were given shelter in a stable. That was where Mary gave birth to her baby boy, Jesus.

In fields near Bethlehem, shepherds were watching over their sheep. An angel suddenly appeared. 'Don't be afraid,' the angel said. 'I bring good news. A Saviour has been born in Bethlehem. He is Christ the Lord. You will find the baby in a manger.'

A choir of angels praised God saying, 'Glory to God in the highest! Peace and good will to all!'

The shepherds found the baby Jesus just as the angel had told them and passed on the good news to everyone they met.

After that, Mary and Joseph travelled with Jesus to the temple. An old man named Simeon held Jesus in his arms and knew that God's promise had been kept. 'I am ready to die,' he said, 'for I have seen God's salvation.'

He then warned Mary that one day she would be very sad: 'A sword will pierce your own soul too.' Mary thought a lot about these things and kept them close to her heart.

A special star guided some wise men from far-off Eastern lands to the place where Jesus was. When they saw him, they fell down and worshipped him. They gave him beautiful gifts.

Because the wise men came from a foreign country, we can know that Jesus is the Saviour of the whole world. Men and women, boys and girls from any country can repent of their sin and trust in Jesus, the Son of God.

When the wise men were warned by God in a dream that there was a plot to harm the baby Jesus, they decided it was best to return home by a different route.

Joseph was warned in a dream that King Herod wanted to kill the baby Jesus. An angel spoke to him: 'Take the young child and Mary, his mother, and go quickly to Egypt. Stay there until I tell you. Herod, the king, is looking for the young child in order to kill him.'

So Joseph, Mary and young Jesus set off on the long journey to Egypt. After King Herod died, Mary and Joseph returned to the town of Nazareth where Jesus grew up, strong and full of wisdom.

But this is not where the story ends. Jesus had been born for a reason. God the Father's plan was that his Son would live a perfect life and die in the place of sinners. Jesus travelled around the country performing miracles and teaching the truth of God before he was arrested, beaten, and killed on a cross.

He did it so that those who trusted in him 'may have life and have it to the full' (John 10:10 NIV).

Mary was close by when Jesus died.
Simeon's warning had come true.
She was very sad.

But Jesus rose to life again.
He triumphed over death, proving that he is God.
Those who trust in him, including his mother Mary,
will also be raised from the dead to live forever with him.

Jesus' risen body was taken back to heaven where he now rules and reigns. One day there will be another journey when Jesus will return to this earth, not as a baby, but as a victorious king.

Christian Focus is for Kids

That means you and your friends can all find a book to help you from the CF4KIDS range – from the very littlest baby to kids that are almost too old to be called a kid anymore.

We publish books that introduce you to the real Jesus, the truth of God's Word, and what that means for boys and girls of all ages.

Reading books is a fun way to find out what it is like to be a follower of Jesus Christ.

True stories, adventures, activity books, and devotions – they are all here for you and your family.

Christian Focus is part of the family of God. We aim to glorify Jesus and help you trust and follow Him.

Christian Focus Publications Ltd,
Geanies House, Fearn, Ross-shire,
IV20 1TW, Scotland,
United Kingdom.
www.christianfocus.com